CHURCH

But Not as You Know It

The time for playing church is up!

**BY
NATASHA ORUMBIE**

Church, But Not as You Know It

Copyright © 2021: Natasha Orumbie

All rights reserved. No part of this publication may be produced, distributed, or transmitted in any form or by any means, including photocopying, recording, or other electronic or mechanical methods, without the prior written permission of the publisher, except in the case of brief quotations embodied in critical reviews and certain other non-commercial uses permitted by copyright law.

First Printed in United Kingdom 2021

Published by Conscious Dreams Publishing
www.consciousdreamspublishing.com

Edited by Savannah McCaster

Typeset by Oksana Kosovan

ISBN: 978-1-913674-53-3

Dedication

This book is dedicated to every soul that is searching for more. You know there is more, but you just don't know how to access it. God wrote this book just for you, and I pray you receive his love and come home.

Contents

Introduction. Where It All Began 7

Chapter 1. What You Thought You Knew 11

Chapter 2. But I Like It Like This! 25

Chapter 3. Change is Hard! 33

Chapter 4. Isn't the Spirit Realm Witchcraft?! 41

Chapter 5. Wait What? I Have a Mandate? 49

Chapter 6. So What Does It Look Like Now? 55

Chapter 7. This Is War! 71

Chapter 8. Where Do We Go from Here? 87

Acknowledgements 101

About the Author 103

INTRODUCTION

Where It All Began

When God first told me that I needed to write this book, I didn't recognise the seriousness of the assignment. I knew I had to share my experience, but I didn't understand why. Who would read it? Who wanted to hear this message? Would anyone listen? But throughout the last few months, God has made it abundantly clear that what I thought about who needed to hear it and why it needed to be written was none of my concern!

When I came back to this assignment, the last edit was November 8th 2020. It is now March 1st 2021, and I seriously got my "marching orders" today, like four times! I could almost tangibly feel God telling me that this was no longer a joke. Someone, I don't know who, maybe a significant number of people, need to hear whatever He is going to have me share over the next however many pages.

If I am truly honest, I realised my resistance and reticence about actually getting down to it, was fear, of which I repent of right now. That fear was the fear of what other people would think. What they would say when they read what I am about to share on these pages? The truth is, what I am about to share is probably going to take many people way out of their comfort zones! It certainly took me out of mine! What I know now, is that I cannot consume myself with anxieties about how this will be received; that part is up to God.

When God gave me the title for this book, "Church – but not as you know it!" it totally resonated and summed up my whole experience. What you are about to explore with me, is a whole new way of experiencing Christ and "church" that may look completely different from anything you have ever lived through. If I'm totally honest with you, at first, I was a little freaked out! It was all a bit too far left, a bit too extreme, and it scared me. But I know that whilst many of you may initially feel that way too, the reason why you're reading this book is that God has ordained for you to do so.

I have prayed, and am praying right now, even while I type, that this book will find itself in the hands of the saint who needs these particular words, for such a time as this. I have prayed that it will unlock something within them that allows them to be open to the many assignments that God has placed on their lives. I pray too, that they will walk in obedience and fulfil the purpose for which they were created. That is my prayer and I trust and believe that it has already been answered. Amen.

CHAPTER 1

What You Thought You Knew

Church

Many of you, like me, will be reading this book having grown up in church all your life. Even if that's not you, however long you've been a believer, I know that we all will already have our preconceived version of what "church" is, and what a relationship with God *is* and what they *look* like. That being said, all I would humbly request, is that you stop what you're doing right now, before reading anything else, and you just ask God to help you be open to hearing another perspective. It doesn't have to be a long drawn-out prayer, just a simple but genuine request for God to help you open your mind to a different way of thinking; because for some of you, what you thought you knew is about to be blown wide open. I don't particularly have an agenda to change your mind about anything in particular, but I do want you to hear me with an open mind, so please, just take a moment and say that prayer. Thank you.

Church had always been for me, a building and the congregational members that attended each week. There was a particular hierarchical order in terms of leadership roles, first the Pastor, then Assistant Pastors, Deacons, Evangelists, Ministers, Worship Leaders and then finally the normal folk! We did things a certain way, in terms of practices that we followed, like starting with Sunday School, then praise and worship, then announcements, then offering, then the sermon, then the altar call and then we're done. Any deviation from that was only "if the spirit leads" and then back in my childhood days, that could mean the entire programme could be completely disrupted, but on those days everyone was just happy that "God had His way"!

Now even if it isn't the exact same format in your church, I'm pretty sure that it will be a pretty similar setup, and in and of itself, of course, there is nothing wrong with that. God is indeed a God of order, but I know for me, I was very much stuck in my ways. As far as I was concerned, it was great if God wanted to "have His way" in the service, but I was very much fixated on the order that I had come to know and love. In reality, if I really get down to it, I had become very

CHAPTER 1. WHAT YOU THOUGHT YOU KNEW

religious about the whole church experience and there was very little depth to it at all.

At the time, I knew nothing different, so it was more than acceptable. For me, church was the building that I went to on a Sunday and again potentially during the week, where I would be able to have access to God in a way that was not really possible at home. At the time, my understanding was that although Jesus was the mediator between myself and God, I genuinely believe that there was a subconscious belief that God only shows up at church, and that is why we attend. Even as I'm writing this now it sounds weird, and I'm questioning whether this was what I ever truly believed or felt, but I believe it was, and sadly it couldn't be further from the truth.

The concept that we, the people are actually the church, and that we make up the very many parts of the body, of which Christ is the head (1 Corinthians 12) and that my 'body is the temple of the Holy Spirit' (1 Corinthians 6:19-20) were notions that, whilst fully aware of them, I very much paid lip service to if I'm honest. I don't think I ever really saw the extension of what Christ could do in the church building/setting could and should be happening to me wherever I am, because I am part of that body even when I am not in the building. I also think it's important that I make abundantly clear here, that I am not advocating in any way shape or form that we don't need to attend a church building, because the scripture endorses the very opposite in Hebrews 10:25. What I *am* saying, however, is that that is not where it ends. As we leave the building, we should be expecting and actually experiencing the real and tangible manifestation of God in our lives and bodies, wherever we are, because God is not restricted to operating from a building.

Prayer

What I thought I knew about prayer…where do I start? Okay, let me go with the basics. What I knew was that prayer was talking to God. I knew, and I have to say *in theory*, that I could do it simply by just verbalising my thoughts in a very straightforward and non-elaborate way. I could do this either in my mind or aloud and that was prayer! I believed that I would simply offer this up and that God would hear me and answer me. But what I also realised is that having been brought up in a Pentecostal church, I had subconsciously learnt some inaccurate beliefs about prayer that I'll explain in more detail.

For those of you who have never been to a Pentecostal church, what I am about to describe may be difficult for you to relate to. If you have never experienced this live and in person or grown up around it in the way that I had, it could

CHAPTER 1. WHAT YOU THOUGHT YOU KNEW

possibly be slightly more difficult for you to comprehend. You may have seen snippets and clips on television, but trust me, having the lived experience of this culture, had a serious and I believe quite a negative impact on my beliefs about prayer.

Pentecostal churches are very loud on the whole. There is a lot of shouting, clapping, loud and passionately expressive music, dancing, running and general excitement. When prayer is announced, and the saints begin to pray, it is very different to the experience that one may have in a Church of England or Catholic Church, where prayers are often read and recited either by one person or collectively in a very structured way. This was all I knew and came to accept as *normal* and it is only upon reflection now, that I realise the negative impact that this had had on me because I grew to believe that the only type of prayer that would actually invoke God's presence or His hand, would be these loud vociferous prayers, where emotions were tangible and decibel levels were high!

As a child, I had watched the elders pray and even if they began calmly and orderly with "Heavenly Father God, we come to you today..." a very popular opening, in many cases it would quickly transition into high pitched shouts or screams as the passion and Holy Spirit took over. In my mind, I realise that I had concluded that it was then, and only then that God would *move* in any situation or that He would come in response to our invitation. I had subconsciously come to believe that my more simple, quiet prayers were not *powerful* enough to truly invoke God's presence or His hand and so there was almost zero expectation that *anything* would happen when *I* prayed, especially if it had not been preceded by the screams and shouts to which I had grown accustomed.

Now understand, no-one *taught* me this, and I know I would have been promptly corrected if I had expressed this view to anyone, and in *theory* I did believe that God hears *all* prayers, even the quiet ones, but I would be lying if I had not felt intimidated by the zeal and passion with which the elders in our congregation were able to pray, almost on cue! I believe this was a strategy of the enemy. He was able to convince me that my prayers were not powerful enough or holy enough because they were not shouted or screamed and I did not always burst into another tongue (we will come to that shortly, if you're not sure what that is) that my prayers would have nil or little effect. It was a simple strategy, but it was effective. It caused me to pretty much give up my power, because I believed I had none. Nothing could be further from the truth, but until what I experienced,

CHAPTER 1. WHAT YOU THOUGHT YOU KNEW

what triggered me to write this book, I was none the wiser. But thank God, I finally got my power back!

Prayer is simply communication with God, and it can be done in any format; spoken, written, sung even and those words have power in *any* of these forms. The power is in and through the belief in the name of Jesus, and at that name, every demonic principality and power *must* bow and, in many cases, they don't stick around long enough – they flee! This is why I totally understand why the enemy's number one strategy is to try and stop people from praying altogether, but if he cannot stop that, he will cause them to doubt their power and authority by whatever means necessary. Whether that be comparing their own prayers to that of other saints or simply just believing the lie that a prayer needs to have a particular format and be said in a certain way in order for God to hear and respond. The sooner we can realign our views with God's original intention for prayer, the sooner we can all get our power and authority back!

The Holy Spirit

My earliest memories of the Holy Spirit was loud screaming and running around, primarily by older members of our congregation! It was something I very much observed from the outside looking in, and what I remember about the whole experience was feeling totally isolated from it all.

Despite all the yelling and jumping and cries that "the spirit was moving" I felt nothing on most occasions, except FOMO (fear of missing out)! "How come everyone else can feel something? What was wrong with me?"

What was a really vivid memory was having to – what was described as "tarry in the spirit" – ask to be filled, to no avail. The Holy Spirit felt elusive and alien and definitely not a person with whom I was expected to have a relationship. An entity that would walk with me and be my companion and help me throughout my day-to-day activities. No way! If anything, the Holy Spirit was a scary force that overtook people's bodies without warning and left them flailing around or totally knocked out by the power. I was definitely afraid.

It is no wonder then, why it took me so long in my adult life to actually see the Holy Spirit any differently, from a healthier perspective. That experience had shaped my perception and there was nothing in me wanting any sort of relationship with Holy Spirit. I can't remember any teachings about it other than the Pentecost, that made people speak in unknown tongues that even they didn't know. I mean, the whole thing just totally freaked me out! It wasn't that I didn't believe, oh no, I believed alright – I was just super scared.

CHAPTER 1. WHAT YOU THOUGHT YOU KNEW

One of the other things I also realise prevented me from relating to Holy Spirit in a healthy way is how I was always taught Holy Spirit was a force and *not* a person. Oddly enough, if I had read the Bible for myself, I would have clearly seen that throughout the Bible, Holy Spirit is clearly referred to as having human characteristics and is referred to as 'He' in John chapters 14, 15, and 16 and as the Comforter or the Counsellor. These are all human character traits, but above all, the trinity clearly states that it is three *persons* in one and in Acts 5:1-4, a man who lied to the Holy Spirit is said to have lied to God.

Now, having an understanding of Holy Spirit in His role as a person, it makes much more sense to seek a relationship with Him and ask for His guidance and support and leading, something I had never ever pursued because I was too busy hiding from Him as I was from God, both of whom had been painted to me as scary, powerful entities that would be super disappointed in me if ever messed up. It was a completely unhealthy perspective and one that had prevented me for many years, experiencing what God had truly desired from the outset, an open and honest relationship with Him, Jesus and Holy Spirit.

I can see why the enemy used this ignorance as a key strategy for preventing God's children from ever uncovering this truth because that relationship is key and truly powerful. I now know how integral a relationship with Holy Spirit is to defeating the enemy, and having and living a victorious Christian life! So now I finally got the revelation and I'm walking in my dominion, the enemy is mad, but who cares?! He has his assignment and I have mine, and one thing that is not part of it is walking in the spirit of fear, which was totally the way of life when I didn't have that true relationship with Holy Spirit. So now, let's move forward in this new revelation.

Relationship with God

Similarly to my Holy Spirit experience, I had a very distant relationship with God. My relationship with God the Father, I think if I'm honest, had been based on my relationship with my earthly father. Whilst I had no doubt whatsoever that he loved me, I don't ever remember hearing those words *ever* from my dad. Whether it was cultural, down to his personal experiences of encountering love from his own parents, or something else, my dad had shied away from displaying any sort of emotion or relating to us affectionately and this had a serious impact on my relationship with God.

If you ever met my dad, you'll know that he is a fun-loving, down-to-earth man with an amazing personality – everyone loved my dad, as did my sister and I. This is why I had no idea that there was any sort of 'dysfunction' for want of a better term. There are so many intricacies that are too detailed to explore here, but what I will say is how I related to my earthly father very much impacted how I related to my heavenly father. Just like with my earthly father, I knew God was *good* and *nice*, I just didn't really feel I knew Him that well. That distance made it hard for me to see how much He truly loved me. I know we talk about God 'loving the world so much that He gave His only Son', and of course, that speaks of a totally amazing love that is truly extraordinary, when you actually get to know God's love, in all its fullness, it is incomparable to anything else you have experienced. Throughout the remaining chapters of this book, you will hear the process of how I was able to finally start having a deeper relationship with Abba Father; the relationship that I was ordained to have from the beginning.

I know that it is still a journey for me because it is years of experiences, patterns and behaviours that I have to actually pick apart. There are years of fearing God and feeling as though He was never ever pleased with me because I messed up so many times. It was years of relating to Him only as the judge, and He is definitely that, but He is also Father and Friend and He truly loves me to the core, even when I have sinned and messed up.

When you manage to grasp that love, it hits differently! It is such a reassurance to know that God is not angry with me when I am wrong. He still loves me and has compassion for me and comes in pursuit of me. The words of the song 'Reckless Love' hit me on another level when I had an encounter with His true love. When I listen to that song now, now that I know what His love truly feels like…all I can say is…wow!

If you have never experienced God's love and its power or ever felt His powerful arms wrap around you, I pray that you will have a powerful encounter with His love, so that you can testify to the words of that song by Corey Asbury.

> Before I spoke a word, You were singing over me
> You have been so, so good to me
> Before I took a breath, You breathed Your life in me
> You have been so so kind to me
> Oh, the overwhelming, never-ending reckless love of God
> Oh, it chases me down, fights 'til I'm found, leaves the 99
> And I couldn't earn it
> I don't deserve it, still You give yourself away
> Oh, the overwhelming, never-ending, reckless love of God
> When I was Your foe, still Your love fought for me
> You have been so, so good to me

CHAPTER 1. WHAT YOU THOUGHT YOU KNEW

> When I felt no worth, You paid it all for me
> You have been so, so kind to me
> Oh, the overwhelming, never-ending reckless love of God
> Oh, it chases me down, fights 'til I'm found, leaves the 99
> And I couldn't earn it
> I don't deserve it, still You give yourself away
> Oh, the…

I'm not sure of your historical experience or views about church, prayer, Holy Spirit and having a deep relationship with God, maybe you relate to some of what I've written in these few pages, or maybe you had a more healthy and balanced view, but I had to set the context for the rest of the book.

I need you to know where I am coming from so that you can appreciate the transition, and some of you may even be able to put yourselves in my position. What I have always known and understood about church had to be unlearnt, as I learned how to pray, love God and have a relationship with Him and Holy Spirit as I come through Jesus the Son, into His presence. What I am about to share has changed me forever, and I pray that as you read these pages, you too will be radically transformed by His love and you will go on to have a lived experience in Him as He intended.

Chapter 2

But I Like It Like This!

I don't know if you can hear the whine in my voice when I wrote the title of this chapter, but believe me, there was a whine! I feel like everyone has this deep resistance to change that causes them to sigh or whine when they're asked to do it! Change takes you out of a place that you may have been for some time, a place that is familiar to you and even if it isn't ideal, it's what you know right? It feels comfortable and you can operate on autopilot, without the need for deep thought and processing. Moving out of one's *comfort zone* is never an attractive prospect! Having to learn something new that you're unsure about, takes effort and time and practice and quite frankly hard work, so I totally get why you may be reading this book and be thinking like that.

I was there too! I attended church regularly, every service, which often meant at least three times a week! When it was Bible Study season, it went up to four times and if there was some other one-off programme, like a Concert or some other kind of event, I could be in church five times for the week y'all! By any standards, five times a week at church is a lot – and even if it were just the three times, I felt like that was a good chunk out of my week…a reasonable *sacrifice*, right? You see that is what I had convinced myself, that I was "doing my bit" and that I was "a good committed Christian". The fact that I attended all the programmes and was involved in multiple ministries within the church setting gave me a certain sense of satisfaction, for want of a better word. I almost felt as though I had definitely *earned* my way into the good books, even though I knew in theory, from the Bible (Galatians 2:16 and Ephesians 2:8) that it was not by works and only by faith that you are justified.

But I believe that the reason it gave me that sense of satisfaction was that the enemy wanted me to leave it just like that! If he could get me so busy ticking boxes and jumping through the proverbial hoops of programmes and service attendance to make me feel that I was doing more than enough to *earn* God's favour, then he was good with that. He didn't have to worry about me, because I was not a threat to him or his kingdom while I was preoccupied with the unimportant.

CHAPTER 2. BUT I LIKE IT LIKE THIS!

Now, don't get me wrong, please hear me! I'm not saying church attendance is not important or being in ministry is not important at all! It is *very* important! A church cannot function if the congregation is not serving in their respective capacities, but where I lost my power and the ability to become a serious threat and opposition to the kingdom of darkness, is because that is *all* I was doing! I knew no other way – I didn't know there was anything else and to be honest, this felt like I was doing great! God would be happy with all the *stuff* I was doing and so would the church leaders and that *had* to be making the devil mad right? Wrong!

None of that stuff had any impact on the kingdom of darkness at all! The enemy is totally fine with us going to church, singing a few songs, fellowshipping with the brethren, having an emotional experience and then jumping right back into our regular lives! That does not affect him or his activities in any way. In fact, did you know he will even encourage you to do even more things, to keep you so busy and distracted from what matters the most – building a deep and true relationship with God and Holy Spirit and finding out your true and powerful identity? Because, you see, when you discover that....that is when you become powerful and *that* is when you are a real threat and it is at this point that you will potentially start to face opposition that will disrupt your status quo!

Now if you're anything like me, you'll be reading that and thinking, why would anyone want to do that then? Why on earth would you want to go from a life of relative peace and comfort to put yourself in the line of fire, right? Who does that? Why would you do that? If you go back to my whiny voice right at the start of the chapter, that whining voice would continue to say, "I don't want any trouble! I don't want to pick a fight with the enemy! I want an easier life!" And please don't pretend like you don't want one too lol! No one likes fighting!! But what I came to realise, is that when we accept Christ, we enter warfare whether we like it or not, and believe me, the comfort zone that I've just described above is one of the enemy's most well-used and hugely successful weapons in his arsenal! Keep them busy, distract them from taking their own weapons out because if they do, we're done for!

His objective is to keep us comfortable, keep us feeling like everything is cool and that we don't have to worry about doing more, and believing we're doing enough. He wants to keep us believing that by doing all of these things we are really hurting the enemy and he is defeated and weakened through those things alone! He is busy faking his death so that you stop worrying about him so that he can continue to work on his strategy to make you weaker and more ineffective as each day goes by. His plan is to keep you so focused on going through the motions that you even forget why you're doing what you're doing. You lose the passion and zeal with which you used to serve, and it becomes a chore and a burden.

That is when he can gradually start whispering to you, "They don't appreciate you! Look how hard you work, look how committed you are and what thanks do you get?" He starts to sow seeds of bitterness and resentment and have you serving with the wrong heart and then he's in! Then he has the legal right to start taking you down that slippery slope and before you know it, you're in church but it means nothing to you. You're serving but it means nothing to you. You're hearing the word, but it means nothing to you. You're involved in every programme, at every event, on every impact team, but it means nothing to you.

It's a slow fade my friend, and all of this starts happening because, from the very beginning, we were satisfied with the status quo. We didn't want more of God because that meant more work! The enemy would whisper gently, "Getting up early to pray? Like every day? That's a lot! And besides, God doesn't need that, He only needs you to acknowledge Him at the start of the day, He knows your heart! He knows how busy you are, He knows you need to rest! God doesn't need all that time!" Do you hear him? Do you hear the enemy's voice? Do you hear how he operates?

The enemy's strategies have not changed. He has been doing this from the very beginning! He comes to you with what sounds like truth, partial truth that he has twisted for his own benefit because this will disarm you and make you less of a threat. Yes, it is of course true that God does understand when you're tired and He very much knows our hearts but the enemy knows that if you spend more time with God daily, things are going to change. He knows that when you spend time in God's presence, Holy Spirit will come and start revealing to you; things of the spirit. Holy Spirit will reveal where you are in sin and have things in common with the enemy for which you need to repent, which will remove the enemy's legal right to have access to you and your life. He knows that once you have repented, Jesus comes in as your mediator and takes you right back to where you are meant to be, into the presence of God, where Holy Spirit can minister to you and empower you and strengthen you in readiness to be able to attack the enemy and his kingdom. Just like in the beginning, his goal is to make you take an action that separates you from the close relationship with God that you were intended to have because it is only when you have that relationship that you get your power!!

CHAPTER 2. BUT I LIKE IT LIKE THIS!

So maybe you were whining like me about liking it the way it is, and I'm hoping you hear now exactly *why* you "like it like this" and why the enemy's plan is continuing to get you to "like it like this", so he can prevent you from accessing what God has for you. Whether you will allow him to succeed, is up to you.

CHAPTER 3

Change is Hard!

I totally get it! Of course, it's hard! Change is never easy, for all the reasons that I laid out in the previous chapter, but with the grace of God, there comes an ease that will help things *feel* easier than they actually are.

I went through a radical change over the months before starting to write this book, changing everything from how I read the Bible, to how I spent time communing with God each day. It was totally alien at first and initially felt quite awkward, for want of a better word, but I have been totally transformed by the process and now feel incredible. It may have been hard, but it was totally worth it!

Change first started for me after what I can only describe as experiencing supernatural healing. If I have to cut a very long story short, a lady by the name of Somalia Brown reached out to me after seeing me very emotional on an Instagram Live. It was totally off-brand and I didn't want to do it at all, but I believe God had me show up in my vulnerability in order for me to get healing. It was not long after the George Floyd killing and like many other members of the black community, I had been massively triggered. It had stirred up for me a hornet's nest of prejudicial treatment that I had experienced throughout my life, which largely started once I had entered the workplace.

I told of example after example where I had been treated unfairly and victimised as a consequence of my skin colour. I shared examples of how I had witnessed this behaviour being done to children, in the education sector and how I had to watch helplessly as the system penalised them, simply on account of their race. I was broken and angry and it literally all came out. Somalia was watching the Live, which was not her normal practice, and she reached out directly to me after the Live offering to pray for me.

Now I had been schooled on being very careful of who I allowed to pray for me! I remember the scripture, "let no man lay hands on you suddenly!" Even though I don't even think that scripture was in the context of the way it was being used – as a warning to avoid random people praying

CHAPTER 3. CHANGE IS HARD!

for you. I don't know why, but I very willingly allowed Somalia to pray for me. During that prayer, she had asked me what was wrong with my throat. I was stunned – how did she know that? Unbeknown to Somalia, because I had only just met Somalia on Instagram over the past year, I had been experiencing ongoing issues with my throat for the past 20+ years. I had even had to have surgery and it all began after that first painful experience that I had shared on my IG Live. Those issues had continued for years, and even at that present time, I had a continuous irritating scratch in my throat, causing me to need to repeatedly clear my throat.

What Somalia had picked up on in the Spirit was that I had been holding on to the unforgiveness towards all the people in the past who had hurt me and as a result, I had opened a door to the enemy, giving him legal right to attack my body in this way. Now I have to tell you, this freaked me out no end! I was like, who is this woman? How did she know that? And I have to confess, it crossed my mind, was she a witch?! I know, I know, I laugh about it now with Somalia, because I know she is far from a witch and just an incredibly powerful woman of God! Now, that was not where the miracle ended! So, she identified this problem, called it out and took me through a process, which I now come to know as going to the Courts. I'll explain more about this in the coming chapters, but in this process, I repented for my unforgiveness towards those who had hurt me, I forgave myself and I literally removed any legal right that the enemy had to attack my body by removing anything I had in common with him and his kingdom from within me, and guess what? I was totally healed! The scratching throat went and the problems I was experiencing with my voice, all gone! Just like that!

Now while I was happy I was healed, for me, it was still a very out of the ordinary experience that I was not quite comfortable with. I still thought Somalia was just…a bit weird, especially when I saw her on IG Lives, saying that we Christians had to take up our spiritual posts in the earth and start praying in our "territories" and stopping the enemy from being victorious through the COVID-19 virus, and preventing the disease from spreading in our area… Territories? Preventing COVID? Was that even possible? It all sounded a little too far left for my liking. Even the wording sounded so super spiritual to me, "territories?! Taking dominion of our territories?" I don't even know why, but it all seemed really weird to me! But I know that is exactly what the enemy wanted. He did not want me to start this process of change in my perception and understanding of who I was in Christ and my role in the Kingdom of God, because he knew that as soon as that happened…it was all over.

CHAPTER 3. CHANGE IS HARD!

So, after that experience, Somalia had occasionally checked in to see how I was doing and whether or not I had had any backlash as a result of the stand I had taken. What was also happening, was that I was identifying other areas in my life that had come up for me, where I also recognised that I had given the enemy ground and it seemed like I was spending my time in a continuous state of repentance! I had a heightened sensitivity to my thoughts and actions, and I was catching them and repenting for them, regularly on a daily basis. I was seeing changes in myself, my workplace, my home, my marriage, my children, literally every area of my life was literally being transformed. It seemed like every week there were more changes! It was crazy, but I liked the changes I was seeing. Although it seemed like a lot of discipline to be continually aware of these areas and actively rebuking the issues, the changes I was making were radically changing my life!

But the real change began in August when I began the "Awe Fast". When Somalia invited me on the Awe Fast, I asked her what it was. She said she couldn't really explain it, but it would be a time for seeking God's face over the space of 51 days covering a little before and a little after the 10 days of awe featured in the Bible. At the time that I said yes, if I'm honest, I really didn't understand what they were, and the little that I had looked up about the Hebraic calendar and appointed times where God would meet with His people seemed a little bit 'out there', but I had had so much experience of God moving in my life in a way that I had never experienced before over the past few months that I was curious and hungry for even more. I felt confident that if it wasn't for me, or if Somalia or anyone else involved was doing anything weird, God would point it out to me! Well, that was my prayer at least. I have to admit, despite all the powerful prayers and interaction that I had had with Somalia, there was still a degree of scepticism in me that wouldn't really go away. I know now exactly why! The enemy did not want me to continue praying and seeking God in this way! His time was short and he knew it!

I felt God giving me permission to get involved. I mean, how could fasting and praying be a bad thing? If I'm keeping a spiritual eye open to any strategic assault, if this was the enemy trying to trick me and get me into some madness, I'm going to spot him a mile off! This was seriously my thought process! I was almost waiting for him to show up lol! But I think you already know that he didn't, well not in that way anyway.

So, the Awe Fast is where the real change began. The first challenge was that we had to have a strict bedtime so that our bodies were rested and we could be strong enough to

CHAPTER 3. CHANGE IS HARD!

get up and pray each day. Now in the US EST time zone, where Somalia was, they were getting up at 1 am to do these prayers, which was 6 am for us, so not as taxing for me, but when I first heard the proposal that we had to be in bed by 10 pm, I was horrified! 10 pm?? I was a self-professed night owl! That was when I got my best work done! I was so busy during the day, working a full-time job, how else would I be able to get my business work done if I was going to bed at 10 pm?? I thought it was ridiculous and it really put me off doing the whole fast, but I decided to go ahead.

The next, excruciatingly difficult part for me was that we each had to have something that we believe God would have us to sacrifice and fast from over that period too, something that would be a real struggle. The first thing that came to me was my sweets! I mentioned it briefly to Somalia and then quickly retracted it and said I would find something else because that would be too difficult. She laughed and said, it was highly likely that God would choose that and sure enough, it was as clear as day that sugar would be the additional sacrifice I would fast from!

Now in addition to the bedtimes and the sugar elimination, the fast was also basically a Daniel fast, so we were eating only vegetables, no processed foods with sugars and drinking only alkaline water, all as a way of detoxing our bodies, which would also equip us and prepare us for this spiritual journey that we were about to embark on. Again, this just felt so extreme! I had never done anything like this before and it was all super new to me. But again, how I had experienced God at move in my life over the past few months was the perfect advertisement. I simply wanted more of Him and if this was a way to get that, I was in!

Chapter 4

Isn't the Spirit Realm Witchcraft?!

I don't know how many of you came from backgrounds like mine, where growing up in the church, we were taught to leave the enemy, Satan, demonic entities, well alone! We were almost taught to fear him, even though the Bible expressly tells us that "God has not given us the spirit of fear, but of power, love and of a sound mind" (2 Tim 1:7) and that "no weapon formed against us shall prosper." (Isaiah 54:17) But even with all of that backing, it was still instilled in us that we better steer clear of the enemy! Don't say his name too loud because he will come to get you!

We just didn't even talk about Satan, let alone discuss how to stand against an assault from his kingdom of darkness. As I said, it was very clearly suggested that if we went up in a fight against him, we had a high likelihood of losing! That thinking and that ideology followed me into adulthood and so when I began to have supernatural experiences and encounters while on the Awe Fast, I was well and truly freaking out! I was very concerned that I was totally stepping out of a safe comfort zone into the middle of a warzone and I was not feeling that at all!

Well, as you know, at the beginning of the Fast I got clearance from Holy Spirit that it was okay to go ahead with the Fast and that I should be obedient to everything that was asked of me over the course of the next few weeks. Now each day, the calls would last from 6 am all the way until 11 am sometimes, but at a minimum, they were at least an hour, more often than not 2-3 hours. Each day, we would go into prayer virtually in our own homes and as we were praying, I would often feel the tangible presence of God in a way that I cannot describe. It was like nothing I've ever experienced before. No whooping, hollering, screaming or shouting from anyone trying to whip me up into a frenzy (disclaimer – not dissing that by the way, just saying it didn't take any of that!) just a heavy, powerful presence of God falling down and ministering to me. I often remained in tears for the majority of the call, unable to do anything but cry and speak in tongues and just receive. I had never felt anything like it.

CHAPTER 4. ISN'T THE SPIRIT REALM WITCHCRAFT?!

I was having a supernatural encounter with God on the calls during the day, but what was also crazy was the powerful and prophetic dreams that I was also starting to have at night. Now I have never been a dreamer. If and when I did dream, I would promptly forget whatever it was I dreamt when I tried to recall it the next day. But during this fast, I was recalling *everything* I had dreamt, like literally everything, including on many occasions, the full interpretation directly to me or via someone else on the call! When what I had dreamt was confirmed through the prayers God had been leading Somalia to pray or something else that had been said on that day, I began to see that this was serious! God was not playing at all and this was the time that He was going to open my eyes up to a whole new world! I now started to realise why these days were called the "days of awe", and how in this period, this appointed time, it seemed like God really was showing up in a way I had never ever experienced.

Now going back to the title, I have to tell you the root of my association with the spirit realm being 'witchcraft' and why, when Somalia was able to discern the connection between the issues in my throat and my unforgiveness, I thought she may have been a witch! It's simply because, in my mind, the only people who ever did powerful acts like that or were able to have accurate spiritual insight must be demonic! Whenever I used to see magicians on the television doing crazy magic tricks and walking on water and things like that, it was seen as something that had to be demonic because Christians or normal people just don't have that kind of power!! Oh my goodness! What a lie from the pit of hell!

God was beginning to open my eyes during these days of awe to give me a fresh revelation of what I have read in the Bible for years and simply overlooked as a simple Bible story, not realising that I was actually witnessing the first-ever demonstrations of supernatural power right from the beginning and who was wielding and showing up with that power? God Himself and also through His Son Jesus and Holy Spirit. Supernatural acts of power were not only normal, but they were used by God *first*! Satan and his kingdom can only try and emulate what God does and as usual, instead of just copying straight out, he often twists and perverts these acts for his own evil purposes.

To help those of you who may have been in the same camp as me, I am just going to take you through a few of the examples that God walked me through as He sought to remind me of what I had read a zillion times, but for the first time, saw with totally new eyes!! Let's start at the beginning, shall we? The first supernatural act, the creation of the world!! Yes! We have read this so many times, but for some reason, it didn't even come across as supernatural, it was just something that

CHAPTER 4. ISN'T THE SPIRIT REALM WITCHCRAFT?!

God did! But I tell you this, speaking a whole planet into being with just your words, is supernatural guys! I don't think I'm going to need to convince you about that, it's not normal! Like who does that?! Then you have making a human out of the ground! Like, really? Normal? I guess not! Supernatural baby! That is what you call supernatural at its finest! Then putting someone into a deep sleep, taking one of their bones and forming another human being? Come on now!

God continued to show me example after example, before Jesus was on the scene, of not only this supernatural power being demonstrated by God, but also how He gave this same power to us as human beings! Now hear me, before you start freaking out, as I did when there was even the suggestion of this! I repelled it! I would say that it isn't for us to have that power, that is God's power and, in my mind, anyone that was talking about having power was New Age and trying to be a god in their own right! I ran a mile away from any such theology! But God began to open my eyes to the fact that not only did He tell us several times in the Bible that He has given us this power to use for the purposes of His glory, but that the enemy was deliberately trying to blind us to the fact that we have this power because as I've said before, as soon as we have this knowledge, that's when we become more powerful through God and become a genuine threat to the kingdom of darkness!

Before I go any further, I want to show you guys the scripture references and encourage you not just to listen to me but go and read these for yourself and ask God to reveal His true intentions for us to you. Read all of the scriptures in context and see with your own eyes what God has been saying to us all along and why the enemy has been actively trying to hide this from us all along! This, my friends, is his most fearful time! When we finally realise who we are in God and the power that has been invested in us to trample the enemy underfoot; that is when it is show time!!

Before Jesus came on to the scene, we have Moses for example. First, we see a burning bush, that is not consumed, that's talking....Um, I don't think you can get more supernatural than that!! Shortly after that, in Exodus 7:10, he is told to go into Pharaoh and throw his rod down, "and Moses and Aaron went in unto Pharaoh, and they did so as the LORD had commanded: and Aaron cast down his rod before Pharaoh, and before his servants, and it became a serpent." Say what?? But in the very next verse, you see something that is key! What the enemy has always done from the start is to copy! The exact same supernatural act is then replicated by Pharaoh's sorcerers! "Then Pharaoh also called the wise men and the sorcerers: now the magicians of Egypt, they also did in like manner with their enchantments." (Exodus 7:11) This is crucial for us to understand! The enemy cannot create! He can only copy and distort! Everything on earth was created by God and was good and perfect! When the enemy comes in, he sees what God does, takes it, copies it and twists it!

This was mind-blowing for me! For my entire life, I was of the opinion that all supernatural acts and activity was demonic. My acceptance of the supernatural ended with my healing and I guess speaking in tongues, but anything else? Nah, that was the devil's territory, nothing for Christians to be stepping into and this is exactly the way the enemy would like it! Leaving me and other Christians in this state of ignorance meant that we would leave him well alone instead of taking dominion against all principalities and powers like we can and should! Exodus goes on to detail account after account of clearly supernatural activity! All of the plagues could not have been explained by anything else. They started and stopped just as quickly, triggered only by the command of Moses and his rod and these are not the only examples.

The examples continue of course in the New Testament, as Jesus performs miracle after miracle, healing the sick, raising the dead... I mean come on people, this is clear evidence! Then when the scripture goes on to say in Ephesians, 1:19-20 that he has placed in us, "the exceeding greatness of His power toward us who believe, according to the working of His mighty power which He worked in Christ when

He raised Him from the dead and seated Him at His right hand in the heavenly places," The supernatural power that raised Christ from the dead resides in us!! We have been given the supernatural power and authority, "to trample on serpents and scorpions, and over all the power of the enemy, and nothing shall by any means hurt [us]." But yet, I was taught to be afraid of the powers of darkness and *this* is why Christians are experiencing so much defeat in their lives.

We do not know who we are!! 2 Corinthians 10:4 says, "For the weapons of our warfare *are* not carnal but mighty in God for pulling down strongholds," our weapons are mighty *in God*! There is nothing about us that is mighty! We can do nothing without Christ but we can do "all things" if we believe, because "all things are possible to him who believes." (Mark 9:23) I was finally satisfied that not only did the supernatural exist, but it was more rightfully belonging to God and the children of God than it is to powers of darkness! They have stolen from us, and it's time to take our power and authority back!

CHAPTER 5

Wait What? I Have a Mandate?

---※☙❦☙※---

This was genuinely news to me! I knew we all had the one mandate, the great commission that everyone knows right? "Go into all the world and preach the gospel to every creature. He who believes and is baptized will be saved; but he who does not believe will be condemned. And these signs will follow those who believe: In My name they will cast out demons; they will speak with new tongues; they will take up serpents; and if they drink anything deadly, it will by no means hurt them; they will lay hands on the sick, and they will recover." (Mark 16:15) This was another confirmation of the supernatural element but that's not what we're talking about here. I want to talk about our purpose, our predetermined purpose for which we were created. If you look up 'predestination' scriptures, you will see that it is abundantly clear that we *all* have a clearly established purpose on this earth, which was identified in our books before we were even born! 2 Timothy 1:9 states that God "saved us and called us to a holy calling, not because of our works but because of his own purpose and grace, which he gave us in Christ Jesus before the ages began," and this is for *everyone*!

I started to come to terms with the fact that my life had a greater purpose and calling after reading John Bevere's book, 'Driven by Eternity'. When I read that book and realised that I did not want to be serving God just because I didn't want to go to hell and that God cared not just about *what* I did, but the motives behind what I did. I suddenly realised that I didn't just want to *barely* make it to heaven, I wanted to make God proud of me and be pleasing in His sight; not for any reward or accolade, but simply because I loved him immensely and I wanted to be everything that He wanted me to be.

I had cried out to God and prayed after reading that book that my life would have purpose and that I would know what God had called me to do and that I would find that out as soon as possible so that I could begin in earnest. I genuinely believe that it was after reading that book that I started to walk fully into His purpose for my life and I am

CHAPTER 5. WAIT WHAT? I HAVE A MANDATE?

now discovering, one assignment at a time, just what it is that He has called me to do!

Now, I know that many of you reading this book are probably starting to wonder now, what is your own God-given assignment? Do you know it? Are you living it? How will you know? All very relevant and valid questions and to be honest, at the time, I don't think I had a clear definitive answer on what I felt my assignment or mandate was, but the most important thing was that I didn't stop! I didn't wait around trying to work out what to do, I just prayed and carried on doing whatever my hands found to do with all my might and at that time, it was working my day job in the Council and then helping to support other baking business owners at the same time as building my own cake business, so I just continued to do that.

As I did so, I could clearly start to hear God more and more tell me what to do in the business. He was directing me on what courses to create, what to call them, how to show up on the platform, what to speak about on my Instagram (IG) Lives, I mean it was like He was the boss and I was the assistant and I was loving it! His ideas were always way better than mine and they seemed to just flow naturally. As I looked at things that I thought, I asked myself: "Why have you done it like that Tasha?" Only to look a little later on at how it perfectly aligned to everything I was doing in a way that I don't think could even be planned! Incredible!

Even at this stage, it felt like this was definitely my purpose and I began to see how all of my previous experience had lined up to this season and moment in time and because of that, I was fully ready to walk into what God had for me! But then suddenly, things began to shift. More and more God had me being more explicit about Him and my beliefs on my Instagram page, which would totally have been a no-no in times previous. As far as I was concerned, my faith is my personal life and it simply cannot be mixed with business, I mean how unprofessional! I laugh now because God clearly had other plans!

I remember distinctly when God told me I had to entitle my IG Live, "Supernatural Business", I was like, "Are you serious God? People will switch off! I'm trying to increase the numbers of viewers in my lives not reduce them!" but the instruction was clear and so I was obedient! In that Live, I didn't even do a call to action to buy something, but straight afterwards someone sent me a message, telling me the Live was *exactly* what they had needed to hear and purchased my highest ticket offer at the time! It was crazy! And instance after instance where out of obedience, I did things that took me totally out of my comfort zone, and closer to the version

CHAPTER 5. WAIT WHAT? I HAVE A MANDATE?

of the business that God was busy creating, He proved to me that if I was obedient and put Him and His objectives before everything, then He would ensure my business was successful; so I started to listen.

God began to reveal to me that He was building Himself a platform. The popularity that I had attracted and followers that I had amassed were not merely as a result of me having an infectious personality and good content, but it was because God was setting the scene and it was not about me...at all. You see I had a mandate! I was right here in this time and space, to minister to particular individuals that He was sending to me. He was calling me to minister and to be the answer to some of the prayers that they had prayed, and what I realised is that if I had not made myself available, these people's blessings would have been delayed.

We all have our own mandate(s). I say plural, because mandates are not permanent and as situations and circumstances change, so may our mandate. Our mandate or assignment may be an individual, a workplace, a sickness, so this is why we have to constantly be seeking His face so He can reveal it along with any changes, because it may not be through our businesses, as you've seen here.

So, I want you to think of your own lives, maybe you are already super clear on this and you can just pray to make sure you stay on point, but maybe it is an area that you are not confident about and I really want you to not go past this chapter until you hear His voice and have a clear perspective.

CHAPTER 6

So What Does It Look Like Now?

Needless to say, I was unable to go back to business as usual. Everything was different, it felt different, *I* felt different and I knew that I wanted to stay in this place, getting to know more and more about God and getting closer to Him. Now I'm hoping that you stopped at the end of the last chapter and sought to hear for yourself what He is calling you to do, but even if you don't have it yet, this chapter will help you get closer to that point. I am going to share the difference between my Christian walk before and my walk after this encounter with God during this season.

Prayer Life

The first radical change was in my prayer life. I had always struggled to pray for a "long" time on my own. Considering that prayer was just a conversation with God and that I was never short of words outside of prayer time, I should have found this to be quite odd. Instead, it became a very much accepted norm that I would either do very short prayers that didn't really give me an opportunity to truly petition God in a way that would have made my prayer life more impactful and this did not bother me in the slightest.

Now don't get me wrong, please hear me, when I make reference to short prayers, I am not saying that anything is wrong with short prayers – not at all. God hears all prayers that are prayed earnestly, but what I mean is that considering all that should be on my prayer list, even a sentence or two on each topic would generate much longer prayers than those I had been accustomed to praying!

I realise now that once again the enemy was at work and there were lots of things involved! You see, when the enemy is trying to attack you in a particular area, he goes innnnn!! And that is not a typo, I need you to hear the exaggeration on that "in" because I need you to understand how many angles he will come at you in, for just one area in your life. With respect to my prayer life, the enemy:

- Had me doubting that my prayers made that much difference anyway (doubt/unbelief = access/open door)

CHAPTER 6. SO WHAT DOES IT LOOK LIKE NOW?

- Had me thinking my prayers were not as good as someone else's who prayed differently, namely those older saints in my childhood who prayed screaming and shouting at the top of their lungs and therefore they could never be as effective (doubt/unbelief = access/open door)

- Had me rushing my prayer time and not being strategic about what I was praying about, therefore leaving several areas of my life totally defenceless and not covered against assaults from his kingdom (no prayer = access/open door)

- Had me viewing God as unsympathetic and unapproachable, which made me not enjoy communion with Father God as I should have (poor relationship/ not knowing who I am in God = vulnerability)

On so many levels, and many more I could go into, he was strategically ensuring that I make a minimum impact in my prayer life. Why? Because he knows full well, that if I start praying, properly, his days are numbered! The power that I will immediately have access to once I start to pray significantly threatens his kingdom. Therefore, his ultimate goal is to get us either not to pray at all, or to only pray very shallow prayers, missing out on several important areas that need Holy Spirit covering and to allow any area such as unbelief, doubt or fear to come in so that he immediately has a legal right to access our lives and trust me, he is on the watch for those doors to open! "Be sober, be vigilant; because your adversary the devil walks about like a roaring lion, seeking whom he may devour." (1 Peter 5:8) He watches and waits for his opportunity because his time is short.

Now, I am ashamed to admit, but I have to be real because I know many of you will relate! There were many days where I barely prayed, if at all! This literally meant that my life was wide open for the enemy to attack my finances, my marriage, my health, my children, my work, like literally all areas were completely defenceless on many occasions. This is a big deal! We wonder as Christians sometimes why so much is happening to us and why we are experiencing so much hardship/heartache in our lives. I have to say that on many of these occasions, we could have avoided some of these experiences if we learned to pray more.

There is power in prayer!! I used to hear this so much as a child. It was one of those buzz terms that got everyone saying "Hallelujah!" and "Amen!" but I wonder how many people genuinely realise just how much power is available to us immediately when we learn how to pray. Over the course of the last few months, God enabled me to see with my own eyes just how much power had been given to me as a believer through the medium of prayer. The key element

CHAPTER 6. SO WHAT DOES IT LOOK LIKE NOW?

was to pray *believing*, because otherwise, we can't expect to receive anything! The Bible reiterates many times that when we pray, we must "ask in faith, with no doubting, for he who doubts is like a wave of the sea driven and tossed by the wind. For let not that man suppose that he will receive anything from the Lord; *he is* a double-minded man, unstable in all his ways." (James 1:8)

God showed me how, through prayer, I could literally render attacks from the enemy powerless with immediate effect. I remember my first experience of it was when I had one of those crazy migraines that feel like they are in your eyes as well! My head was pulsating and I thought it was going to blow up! I decided I was going to try out what I had been learning and I touched my forehead and I commanded the headache to go immediately and instantly, I was healed! I was so excited! I couldn't believe it! I suddenly realised that if I really believe and my request is in line with His will, then it's a done deal!

I was super excited to try this out everywhere! I tried it out in my home and watched as any wayward attitudes and unwanted behaviours ceased *immediately* and when I say *immediately* I'm seriously not joking! I learnt how to pray with expectation, authority and wholehearted belief and the results were incredible. I'll give you one last example, which hugely excited me! During the course of the last few months, at some point, God healed me of asthma! I had suffered with it for years, diagnosed as having bronchitis from a child. My asthma would be triggered by dust, exercise, even laughing too hard made me sometimes reach for my inhaler! When I realised it had disappeared, I of course told everyone my testimony and I have to say that the enemy did not stop trying to make me doubt and believe I did not have healing, which would have opened a door, but thankfully I have been successful at keeping that door tightly shut! There was one occasion where he was trying really hard! I woke up and I heard an audible whistle from my chest, it was a loud sound and immediately something rose up within me, righteous anger! With no thought, I immediately rebuked the enemy. My exact words were, "How dare you?! Are you mad?! Get out of here, I am fully healed in the name of Jesus and my lungs work at full capacity!" I am telling you now, it was literally seconds! I heard about three more audible whistles and then bam – silence! The enemy got a slap down and I was reminded once again just how much authority we are walking in!

Another of the main changes in my prayer life was creating an altar to God of a carved-out space and time that we would meet regularly. In the Bible, we hear repeatedly that servants of the Most High God would come to Him and there was always an altar involved. Now I know we are not required to build physical altars where we will sacrifice animals and flour, because Christ came to set us free from that element of the law, and ultimately I know that we are the living sacrifice and our lives and prayer itself is the altar. However, what I also realised is that getting out of my bed and escaping to a designated space has massively impacted my prayer time for the better. I now have a little prayer closet under the stairs, and this has really helped me to stay focused and it has been especially useful in a house where there are not that many rooms for you to go off and have solitary time alone, so it has worked a treat!

Relationship with God

My relationship with God has changed massively and I know that this has been as a result of the amount of time I am spending with Him and also understanding more about who He *really* is! Like I have said previously, I have had very distorted perspectives about God and who He is and what He really thinks of me and how I should approach Him.

As a child, I was taught to fear God and that is obviously the right thing to do if we understand what the fear of the Lord looks like. For me, when you fear something you are afraid of it, and when you're afraid of it, you stay away from it! While it lasted, it was a good strategy because it meant

I didn't know how to relate to God the Father and so I felt very far away from Him and like I said earlier, this was a specific strategy the enemy was using.

When I began to understand what *healthy* fear and reverence meant, it really helped me to start accessing God more easily. I started to see that in "the fear of the Lord one has strong confidence, and his children will have a refuge." (Proverbs 14:26) I began to approach His throne of grace with confidence as he told me to in Hebrews 4:16 and I was getting to know my Father rather than just God the Judge!

I don't know about you, but if you came from a church where there is an imbalance in the representation of all sides of God, you may form the same perspective of God and see Him as the Judge only. Daily communion with God has taught/reminded me that God loves me immensely and nothing I can do will *ever* change that! I had always heard and accepted this with my mind but not with my heart. For example, if I had felt that in some way I had let God down and fallen short in my behaviour, then He would be angry with me and so it was something that prevented me from approaching boldly because I was ashamed and felt that I did not have the right to come before Him in my sin.

CHAPTER 6. SO WHAT DOES IT LOOK LIKE NOW?

One thing that has really helped me significantly in this area is the consistency of coming to Him. It makes total sense now that I think about it, because it works the exact same in the natural realm. The more time you spend with someone, the more natural you will find it to speak to them, even if you were strangers before. More importantly, I learned to hear back!! This was a total game-changer for me! Never in my life have I experienced hearing God's voice like I am now. It is almost audible but not quite! However, I can hear loud and clear exactly what He is telling me to do. He will speak to me in the prayer time I carve out during the morning but also throughout the day. I will hear Him tell me to stop when I am about to do or say something, I will hear something specific that I must do or say and likewise when I need to stop and listen, but none of this would have been possible had I not began to consistently carve out that time to meet with and commune with Heavenly Father. I would urge you to do the same and just see how much your relationship will change.

Discipline

Another area of my life that looks totally different now is discipline. I have to admit that I am quite a disciplined person naturally. When I know what needs to be done in any sphere, I am a person that likes to follow guidelines and rules and I am great at sticking with them, but ironically,

I had no discipline in my spiritual walk because I guess for me there were no clear guidelines set out and that left me doing this in a haphazard way.

Bible Reading

If you have the You Version Bible app, you may be familiar with the 'streaks' awards that you get for reading your Bible on consecutive days and weeks and I have to ashamedly admit that my highest streak ever was only 70 something! I definitely read my Bible, but reading it every day was just one of those things that would often get put on the list of things to do that sometimes never got done for one reason or another. With all the best intentions, I realised that for me personally, if I didn't set time aside to read the Bible at the beginning of the day, that it wouldn't happen and so I decided that I was going to have to get disciplined about this. At the time of writing, I'm currently on Streak 68 in days and 69 in weeks, and I know that for the first time this year, I will be able to see a streak of reading my Bible *every single* day by God's grace. And this is not because I've now added Bible reading to the list of rules that must be obeyed in my usual fashion, but because I absolutely understand now how important it is to hear God speaking to me and this is often done directly through His word. I need to be in a place where I am so full of His word that it flows out of me automatically and without effort. I have a way to go but

I know God can supernaturally accelerate me in my journey, so I will continue to remain committed to doing my part as I know God will do His.

Prayer

I've talked extensively about prayer previously but again this needed to become a discipline. Praying about things until you say change is encouraged in the Bible. James 5:16 tells us that "the effective, fervent prayer of a righteous man avails much." and in some versions effective and fervent is replaced with 'persistent'. What God has taught me in this time is how important it is to be disciplined about continuing to pray for things until we see change and I have to admit that this is what I have found the most challenging to do previously and I must actually write down a set list so that I can have the core things that I will pray about consistently listed and then add things to it as I go. Being disciplined about praying for our needs as well as covering the areas of our lives serves as a hedge of protection against the strategies from hell. The enemy's power is limited, and we can cover ourselves through persistent and fervent prayer. My daily time each day has allowed me to do this and I would highly recommend becoming more disciplined in this area.

My Body is a Temple

I have never really been passionate about food. For me, food was a necessity and not a pleasure. I used to say that if I could take my food intake/requirements in tablet form, I would honestly do that! Eating was a chore and cooking definitely was too, so I would often end up eating junk and not considering at all the impact on my body. My worst bad habit – and I have to say addiction, because I realised it actually was – was the consumption of sugar. I consumed so much sugar that my teeth literally were falling out and decaying so badly and the strangest thing was that I didn't care! Can you believe that? I was seriously saying I would prefer to get false teeth than stop eating sweets! A serious addiction and when the Awe Fast required us to ask God what He would want us to give up, aside from the Daniel Fast part, I convinced myself that He would never ask me to give that up because that would be too difficult lol! Alarm bells!! So, you guessed it, that was what I had to give up and I haven't eaten sweets since August 2020 (bar two gummies I had on Valentine's Day), some 8 months! Knowing my addiction to it, I don't think I will ever go back!

Another addiction I had was to work! Yep! I was a self-confessed workaholic and to a degree, I still believe God is working on this area in me! As with many addictions, I believe they are an anaesthetic, numbing a deeper pain/

CHAPTER 6. SO WHAT DOES IT LOOK LIKE NOW?

issue and I am still digging as to what that could be, but what I do know is that God seriously challenged me in the area of rest! One of the Awe Fast specific requirements was to be in bed by 10.30 pm so that we were able to maximise and benefit from the sleep between the hours of 11 pm and 3 am where we have more NREM (non-rapid eye movement) sleep and this is essential for the restoration and healing of our organs. Now when I heard this I was horrified!! I was definitely a night owl and the thought of going to bed at this time was alien to me! It was super early! But God convinced me and I knew that change was needed.

I have to say that it was not easy, but for the whole time of the Awe Fast, I was super disciplined. On the whole, ever since, I have made it a priority to get to bed as close as I can to 10.30 pm, and although there have been occasions where it wasn't possible, in the main, I've been so much more sensible about bedtimes. I can see that God was trying to help me help myself and later still, months after the fast, God challenged me about rest, and brought back the revelation about the Sabbath. Now this is something that I know causes flurries of contention with people having different views and I was in two minds about whether or not to add it into the book because I know that for some people this won't sit well and maybe they won't understand, but I'm sharing it anyway because this has been a deep conviction of mine since God revealed it to me.

I know that the Sabbath teaching is one of the Levitical laws that many believe died with Christ and I agree that the rigidity of the law, the timings the animal sacrifice, all of that, is definitely not relevant now, because Jesus was the ultimate sacrifice that abolished the law. And in Romans 14:5-6, Paul wrote: "One person esteems one day above another; another esteems every day alike. Let each be fully convinced in his own mind. He who observes the day, observes it to the Lord; and he who does not observe the day, to the Lord he does not observe it. He who eats, eats to the Lord, for he gives God thanks; and he who does not eat, to the Lord he does not eat, and gives God thanks."

To me, this clearly suggests that Paul is saying that each person must be subject to their own conviction on this and that ultimately, God will convince some to keep the Sabbath in a particular way and others not. Similarly with food, which is another area that God clearly gave me specific instruction about. In the same way as the days for keeping the Sabbath, God may have you abstain from animal products and others may have no issues there. I am very much convinced that God has asked me not to eat dairy products or meat and I do not know why, but I know what He has asked me to do and therefore that is exactly what I am going to do!

CHAPTER 6. SO WHAT DOES IT LOOK LIKE NOW?

God in all his infinite wisdom knows each of us individually, and knows why he may say to me "I don't want you to watch that movie" and for someone else, it's perfectly fine. This is why the Bible also says in Philippians 2:12, "Therefore, my beloved, as you have always obeyed, not as in my presence only, but now much more in my absence, work out your own salvation with fear and trembling," because each person must be fully convinced of what God has had them to do rather than be reliant on what someone from the pulpit tells you to do, which may be their own personal conviction.

For me, God was clear that I need to keep the principle of the Sabbath, which continues to be reinforced throughout the Bible, before and after Christ's death and that is the principle of rest. I know why for me personally this is something that *I* needed, which is reflected in the scripture when in Mark 2:27, Jesus said, "The Sabbath was made for man, not man for the Sabbath." This statement was in response to the accusation that His disciples were breaking the law regarding resting on the Sabbath when they walked by some fields and plucked heads of grain. (Mark 2:23-28; also Matthew 12:1-8; Luke 6:1-5) I know that I have struggled to rest for as long as I can remember. There was *always something* to do! I could never just sit still and be at peace; I always felt guilty! Sleep was like eating was to me, something that if I could get away with not doing it, I would! It just felt like a waste of time!

This was indeed another strategy that I could see was clearly being maximised by the enemy in my life particularly. You see, if he could exhaust me, and wear me down physically, again I am of less effect in the Kingdom of God as an assault against the forces of darkness and therefore by keeping me busy and wearing me out, he was attempting to eliminate the threat! God reminded me that for *me*, I need to be reminded to observe that principle and that is through getting to bed regularly at a reasonable hour, before 11 pm and ensuring that at least one day per week, I am not doing 'work, work' and just focusing on resetting my body.

I think that is the conclusion of this chapter really, summing up what has changed now, and that is that I have finally learnt that I need to have my own personal relationship with God and that I cannot rely wholly on what someone else tells me about my faith. God speaks to us all if we allow Him to, and now that I spend time daily in communion with God, I get more of a chance to hear His heart and know what He wants both from, and for, me. I would challenge you to consider whether you are hearing from God, or whether when you hear from the pulpit, that you do take it back to God for yourself and see exactly what He is saying to you, individually through that word.

Chapter 7

This Is War!

As I said at the beginning of this book, 'spiritual warfare' is certainly a term that I would have avoided having anything to do with, and I definitely did not anticipate me feeling unafraid of broaching the topic. As I said, I was brought up fearing anything to do with this topic and so what you are going to read in the next few pages is new to me and it may be new to some of you all too.

I want to encourage you all not to be afraid. "God has not given us the spirit of fear, but of power, love and of a sound mind." (2 Timothy 1:7) The forces of darkness and principalities and powers are no match for the power of God and that same power resides in you and me. The enemy is counting on us not knowing who we are so that we do not use the power that we have.

The first time I think I really understood the reality of how spiritual warfare would manifest in the day-to-day reality of every human on earth is when I read C.S. Lewis's 'Screwtape Letters'. If you have not read that book, I urge you to do so! Whilst it is definitely a fictional account, it strikes me as quite an accurate representation of the way in which Satan is seen to have manoeuvred in Bible accounts, and the strategies used by the demonic powers that are detailed in this text certainly do appear quite plausible. Now irrespective of whether one wants to argue about the accuracy of a fictional perspective, I think what is the most important is understanding that "we do not wrestle against flesh and blood, but against principalities, against powers, against the rulers of]the darkness of this age, against spiritual *hosts* of wickedness in the heavenly *places*." (Ephesians 6:12) What we see in the flesh are the circumstances and scenarios that have been planted, orchestrated by the enemy in order to get us to sin. Because the warfare is spiritual, the weapons have to be spiritual too. 2 Corinthians 10:4 reminds us that "the weapons of our warfare *are* not carnal but mighty in God for pulling down strongholds," which in short means that if we are going to win a spiritual war we need to fight with the right arsenal.

CHAPTER 7. THIS IS WAR!

I have seen for myself, even while I wrote this chapter, exactly what that looks like and I almost think God allowed it to happen so that I could write this from a viewpoint that I think will be more helpful to most. He really does work all things together for the good of those "who love him and are called according to His purpose." (Romans 8:28)

One of the disciplines that I had been practicing over the past few months is really meditating on scriptures and at different points in the day, being intentional about coming back to those scriptures to re-read them. I have also been repeating affirmations that remind me of God's promises towards me and what he says about me, and I have found that these practices have significantly elevated me spiritually. I felt stronger, more focused and when the attacks of the enemy came, I was able to not only identify them quickly but fight back, often using the same word that I had been standing on as a weapon.

However, what happened to me this past week was that I became complacent. I thought to myself, "Tasha, you've been building yourself up for so long now, you don't need to get so religious about doing all this Bible reading throughout the day. You read it once at the start of the day, that is enough to get you through; after all, you have so much backlog in your tank, there simply isn't the need. You have so much to get through; constantly interrupting your day in this way is counterproductive and simply unnecessary. Be careful you don't become over-religious about this like the Pharisees!" I wonder, who on earth could have planted these thoughts?! Hmmmm, let me think!!

I couldn't believe it! Just like that! Slick and subtle! My guard came down, he saw an opening and boom! As a result, I became spiritually weak and defenceless against his attacks which came thick and fast, I'm telling you. I was emotional, defensive, frustrated, losing my peace, you name it, this week was a far cry from the contentment and joy that I had been experiencing over the past few months. It had totally summed it up for me and now I realise, more than ever, that this is not a game! Satan is not playing! He has a job to do and even when we forget this, he never does! He is not taking a rest while we get on with destroying his kingdom! Why should he? Who sleeps while someone is trying to break into their home and take their spoils? No one right? But this is exactly what many of us do. If we have forgotten, 2 Corinthians 2:11 reminds us that we will be taken advantage of by the enemy if we remain ignorant of his devices, "lest Satan should take advantage of us; for we are not ignorant of his devices."

CHAPTER 7. THIS IS WAR!

The surprise for me is how easy it was for me to be still caught so off guard, even after all of this training and preparation that I had done and it was then that the Lord gave me this analogy and it was as clear as day! What I had been doing for the past few months was becoming spiritually fit, like an athlete. Initially, while I trained, it was hard to stay committed. Each of the different exercises was intense and required great effort. Taking time out to pray for so long each morning, taking even more time out to continually reflect on His word and repeat affirmations and continually check my heart and my motives. It was exhausting. Just like it is for a new athlete when they begin training.

All the while they train, they are building muscle memory and they become stronger and each exercise begins to become less taxing as your body adapts. Likewise, memorising the scriptures and being so intentional about checking my behaviours and attitudes became almost second nature. Praying during the different watches of the day in this way was giving me the supernatural protection I needed to stand against the wiles of the enemy, just as the athlete who is diligently training will effortlessly be able to stand against the competition.

As God continued to expound on this analogy, He began to show me so many more areas that revealed why this breach in my fortified hedge of protection had been possible. I had started going to bed later again because I "had things to finish". This was impacting on my physical strength, making me more prone to being emotional and irritable and contributing to other behaviours that gave the enemy a legitimate door to go through and have access to my life. It was a slow fade, but I realised that the enemy had no other way to get access to me other than if he made me do it myself! This was mind-blowing for me! I realised right at this point that as long as I stay disciplined and focused on doing the spiritual activities that will keep me spiritually fit, the competition will find me pretty hard to beat! The difficulty comes when I decide to stop exercising and training. That is when all the problems begin! So, let me take you through what I had been doing to keep myself in spiritual shape and the gradual decline that could have been fatal had I not identified the issue and addressed it quickly.

Rest

The first thing that I had been told by God to maintain is rest. This was a big thing for me because the workaholic thing was real! I am still asking Holy Spirit to help me unpack the root of this and I do believe it stems from that desire to be perfect and also the desire to people-please, completing everything that everyone would want from me at any given time. Both places are unhealthy foundations on which to build any lifestyle and so let me be honest and say that this has been an area of struggle but I am declaring right now that it will not be a continual state of mind. I speak total freedom from that bondage right now in Jesus' mighty name. Just as a side note: that is how I handle any negative thought or mindset or other attack, in whichever form it may come. I acknowledge it but do not *own* it! There is a difference. Let me just give you an example below because this is an important point:

- Version 1 – Owning the negativity

    "I am a workaholic and it's all rooted in my perfectionism and people-pleasing tendencies, but I'm working on it."

- Version 2 – Acknowledging but not accepting the negativity

    "In the past, I have struggled with overworking and people-pleasing but I speak total freedom over that bondage right now in Jesus' name. I take dominion and declare that whatever the root of those negative behaviours are, they are destroyed right now and that Holy Spirit will give me the grace to control those behaviours."

Two different perspectives. The minute that we speak version 1, we have given the enemy more access to continue to wreak havoc in that area, whereas version 2 acknowledges he is trying to get in but kicks him back out and bolts the door behind him. In short, I would say that it could be paralleled to this – having the temptation is not the sin, it's *yielding* to that temptation which is where the problems start.

But that was a serious digress! Wow! I was talking about rest and then ended up all the way over here! Clearly, God needed to share that with someone! I agree, I believe it is important to really drive home that my mindset and self-talk have been a key part of the warfare. If we fail to realise how important our thoughts and words are we will continue to place weapons in the enemy's hands that he will happily use to hammer us!

So, getting back to rest, Holy Spirit had made it very clear to me that I was not getting enough rest and basically trying to do things in my own strength. I was not asking for help or grace; I was simply trying to do everything under my own steam. I was a "just get it done, whatever it takes" kind of girl, and I was very confident in my own abilities to just plough through, which was definitely part of the problem. Acknowledging that I need Holy Spirit to lead, guide and assist me would have helped me to avoid the trap of thinking that I will get everything done if I just stay up and work through the night whenever I need to, and quite simply just abuse my body whilst I continue to walk in pride, thinking I can do it all.

CHAPTER 7. THIS IS WAR!

Now don't get me wrong, I'm not saying that you shouldn't work hard, or put in the effort, but what is really important to understand is that if we are dependent on our own strength, it will never be enough. Sleep was designed by God as a part of the model of regular rest that was in place from the beginning of time. After all God's work when He created the heavens and the earth in the beginning, He rested. It is not something that we can choose to avoid without penalty.

So Father had told me that I needed to start going to bed by 9.30 pm so that I can be fully asleep by 10.30 pm latest, especially as I was now getting up at 4.30 am. This was to ensure that I managed to get my business activities out of the way before I began my day job, as well as give me enough time to spend in devotion before my day started in earnest. Now I did really well for some time. But for whatever reason, I broke the pattern one night and it opened a door of complacency.

The enemy had used the exact same strategy that he used on Adam and Eve in the garden! I couldn't believe I fell for it!! I knew what I had been told by God about the bedtimes, but God had also been helping me with becoming overly fixated and religious about finer details simply because, for me, it almost became like I was trying to *earn* my way into heaven through works and following all the rules to the letter! So

Holy Spirit had given me grace when I would occasionally slip, or where there was an exceptional circumstance where I needed to stay up to complete something as a one-off, like a cake or a report, where non-completion is not an option. But what the enemy had tried to do, was convince me that God would be okay with me not keeping to the bedtime because after all, I shouldn't get religious about it, right? He twisted what was a clear instruction to me by God and basically said, "He didn't surely mean that you have to be in bed by 10.30 pm every night? Surely that is not sustainable with all that God has asked you to do right? He wants you to finish X doesn't He, so of course, He will be cool with you continuing to stay up late until it's done?" and just like Eve, I totally fell for it!

I remember I used to cuss Eve and wonder how she could be so dumb as to listen to the serpent over God! I mean, who would do that? *sips tea and looks left to right* So that was it! It was the start of an incredibly slippery slope and just like it is in the natural realm, so it is in the spirit realm. I was not getting enough rest and so I became weak. What I should have done was what Jesus did when He was tempted in the wilderness and used the Word of God to pipe right back up and tell Satan where to go! But maybe I didn't have enough of the right word in me to be able to use it in an attack! This brings me nicely to the next weapon that God gave me to fight the war in the spirit realm and how I gradually lost touch with that too!

The Word of God

You guys have already heard me talk about my previous challenges of being able to read the Bible daily without any real focus and attention. It was a muscle that was definitely underworked, and I was just beginning to start to use it more each day and it was becoming easier! I was finding more in the word and Holy Spirit was opening my eyes to revelations that I had never ever seen and it was incredible.

I had also been introduced to the power of continually digesting the word throughout the day to ensure that it was in me, so that I was comfortable with it and therefore ready to use it as a defensive weapon. It's just like David in the story of David and Goliath (1 Samuel 17) – David was given armour and weapons that he was unfamiliar with and he was very clear that there was no way that he would be able to successfully fight and defeat the giant with armour that he was not used to. It didn't matter how big and powerful the weapons were or how protective the armour was, if he didn't know how to wear it and function in it properly it would probably have been a hindrance rather than a help! What David was comfortable with, was what he was *used to*. He had used his slingshot so many times before to defeat other giants he had faced and successfully defeated because he knew what he was doing with it and he used it regularly.

As the Bible clearly states in Ephesians 6:17, the Word of God is "the sword of the spirit". It is the only offensive part of the whole armour but it is what God has equipped us with to defeat the enemy. The reason why the enemy so often defeats us is that we are unfamiliar with it and don't know how to use it properly! The only way you get more familiar with something is to spend time getting used to it, learning about it, reading up on how to use it effectively, practising using it, all of these things are super important.

I had started to build up my spiritual muscle in that area and was reading Ephesians 1 for example three times per day, and getting it into my spirit and making the words more real to me. At first, it was like I was seeing new things every time I read it and I could feel the words speaking directly to my spirit man, feeding it and as a result, my spirit man was growing in strength. But…over time, my days were getting busier, and I wasn't always able to do the lunchtime read of the scripture and then that started slipping to failing to do it in the night. All the while, I was starving my spirit man of the food it so desperately needed. And just like in the natural realm, the harmful effects of failing to feed your physical body may not be immediately evident, but over time the

CHAPTER 7. THIS IS WAR!

weight starts to fall off and physically you become weaker. In many cases, the consequences will already have had a considerable impact by the time the damage is visible, and while it isn't beyond repair, the damage is done nonetheless.

One of the additional scriptures I was also using to help me in the spiritual war was putting on "the whole armour of God". I was doing it as part of a challenge by the lovely Somalia Brown, putting it on every three hours at the different watches of the day. I simply verbally spoke each piece of the armour and declared what I was protected from and walking into as a result of having the armour on. I had felt incredibly empowered and I could see the impact almost instantly! When situations came up and I would have had negative thoughts, I stopped them dead and readjusted my helmet of salvation and declared that my thoughts were taken captive by the Holy Spirit and that my thoughts would stay on Christ and I would think on whatever was lovely, true and of good report because I was wearing this helmet. I put on the breastplate of righteousness and declared that my heart and my emotions were completely protected by this armour. No more would my emotions control me or manipulate me to behave out of alignment with God's Word and no more would I be subject to their every whim. When I could see myself being triggered emotionally, I would readjust the breastplate of righteousness and get those emotions back in check.

When wearing the belt of truth, I would declare that I would not only walk in the spirit of truth, but I would operate in the dimension of truth daily, enabling me to speak truth as well as discern truth. That I would not be deceived by any of the enemy's falsehoods regardless of means it may choose to present itself and that I would be able to clearly identify any lie from the pit of hell. If I was in a situation where I wanted to assess the validity of someone's claims, I would just remind myself that I am wearing the belt of truth and Holy Spirit will help me to discern appropriately.

Wearing the gospel shoes of peace was a reminder that I do not walk in conflict, but the peace of God is mine and I will take it wherever I go. In any situation, circumstance, or conversation, I will bring an evident peace that will shut down any aggressor and evade any conflict. If I ever felt troubled or restless, I would remind myself that peace is following me, I am walking in the dimension of peace and as long as my mind stays on Christ he will keep me in perfect peace! (Isaiah 26:3)

The shield of faith was my favourite piece, declaring that no weapon formed against me will prosper. (Isaiah 54:17)

CHAPTER 7. THIS IS WAR!

Whatever the enemy tries to throw at me, every fiery dart, will be quenched! He literally cannot touch me as long as I am behind this shield! Do you see how powerful this is? Every attack, every strategy, every assault, cannot succeed IF you have the shield of faith! Do you believe? Or are you doubting whether God can fight for you?! The minute doubt shows up, your shield comes down! At any point where I start to feel insecure or begin to have doubts about anything, I am reminded that I need to raise my shield!

And lastly, the only offensive weapon, as I mentioned before, the sword of the spirit can totally destroy the enemy! It is sharp and it is two-edged, so whichever way you strike, you are doing damage! So, for this one, I am working on having more of God's Word on the tip of my tongue so that I can wield that sword and destroy the enemy when he comes for me!

When I stopped putting on the armour throughout the day, I gradually started to see how I had begun to forget how to defend myself when the enemy was attacking. I was not instinctively adjusting the armour, rather instead, I was succumbing to every assault and losing my victory! It was then I began to see that the slow fade is one of the most dangerous weapons of the enemy. If he can't get you to backslide and turn away from God completely, he will focus primarily on the slow fade, getting you to disarm yourself. If he can make you weaker, you are less able to defend yourself or fight back and you make careless mistakes that give him further legal access to your life!

I realised that Satan and the kingdom of darkness do not take weekend breaks and give you a chance to get your strength back! They are continually on the attack, whilst so many Christians are just coasting along, minding their business, totally unaware of the hijack! When my eyes were opened to this, I started to understand why the Bible tells us that "men ought always pray and never faint", (Luke 18:1) because the "enemy is prowling around like a roaring lion seeking whom he may devour." (1 Peter 5:8) He is only able to devour those who are weak and defenceless and so that is what his objective is to do, make you weak!! This is exactly how it works, even in the natural realm that is how lions operate. They don't go for the strong in the herd, they are too much hard work! They are looking for those who are slower and easier to catch, easy prey. Many of us have made ourselves easy prey to the enemy because we have failed to remember that this is WAR!!

Chapter 8

Where Do We Go from Here?

So, you have read everything I've covered so far and you may be thinking, 'what now?' Well, let me start by saying one thing, do not feel that it's okay to do nothing. *Something* has to change. Until you awaken from this slumber, you will remain stuck and powerless. Only you will know exactly what change is needed, but I'm going to talk you through what I changed, and have to continue to implement in my life that is keeping me going. It is my prayer that it will give you some assistance or at least be a starting point.

If I go back to that analogy of the athlete, as I think it's one to which we can all relate, becoming a successful athlete requires intense hard work and dedication. No athlete, no matter how skilled, can turn up on the day of the race having done no preparation and compete expecting to win or even rank at the very least. We know that success is predicated on having done the hard work ahead of time, the *daily* training, not just training just before they are about to compete, but continually conditioning their bodies to be able to endure. They must build stamina, muscles in the right places, they must eat the right foods, get the appropriate amount of sleep, all of which are required for them to be able to achieve any sort of success in their chosen field.

It is no different for us as Christians, except, unlike the athlete, we do not know when we will need to compete, because our event can happen at any time, unannounced and often, when we least expect, which is why we *have* to be prepared! We *have* to be ready, "in season and out of season" (2 Timothy 4:2), always ready to go when the battle cry sounds. The enemy and his kingdom are doing just that. They are studying our behaviours, weaknesses and flaws and are looking for that Achilles' heel, the area of weakness, the gap in the armour so that they can come in unannounced and take advantage.

The reason why the enemy is so successful at achieving this objective is that most Christians are "ignorant of his devices" (2 Corinthians 2:11), so he is often able to get that advantage. If we continue with the analogy, athletes competing with

CHAPTER 8. WHERE DO WE GO FROM HERE?

one another will study their competitor's races/events and identify their weakness, whether that be how they take the bend, whether they are slow to start, whether they struggle to push far enough at the finish line, they know, and they will hone their strategies to capitalise on the same! So we have to know our enemy, but more importantly, know our own weaknesses and work on them until we have mastered how to conquer them.

Now before we move away from this analogy to translate what this looks like in your spiritual walk, I want to just share this one last thought. Have you ever seen what can happen to an athlete when they stop training regularly, stop eating healthily and start to move away from the strict regimen that kept them fit and competition ready? I would tell you to look up some specific examples but I don't want to call anyone out! However, I'm sure you've all seen it! It is what happens to any of us if we stop doing anything that requires discipline to be maintained? It's a mess! It is no wonder that we end up spiritually unfit. Many of us have gotten out of shape and ultimately this leaves us very susceptible to the enemy's ploys and with very little chance of winning any battles when we are this weak and unfit. So, guess what the enemy's strategy will be? To deter you from the activities that will strengthen your spiritual muscle and render you helpless and vulnerable. The rest of this chapter will lay out my battle plan and I hope that it provides you with a steer on how to effectively stay in shape and equipped to combat the enemy.

Repentance

Living a life of repentance was totally alien to me. As far as I was concerned, I repented when I got saved and unless I backslid, or committed some serious sin, then what was I repenting for? That was my first mistake! You see the Bible clearly tells us that we have "all sinned and fall short of the glory of God", (Romans 3:23) and in fact, we sin daily. We were in fact "born in sin and shaped in iniquity" (Psalm 51:5) and the Word says our very hearts are "deceitful above all things, and desperately wicked: who can know it?" (Jeremiah 17:9) So this basically confirms that not one of us can act as though we are sinless and we need to set a watch against sinning in our lives for a very good reason. Other than the fact that we are commanded to "be holy" because God is holy (1 Peter 1:16), when we sin, the enemy has a legal right to access our lives! He is the accuser of the brethren but he actually isn't lying about us! What he accuses us of are actual sins we have committed that we have not repented over and sought forgiveness! He is therefore fully entitled to approach the Courts of Heaven and make an accusation to God, the righteous judge, against us!

CHAPTER 8. WHERE DO WE GO FROM HERE?

In order to render those accusations powerless, we need to quickly agree with our adversary in Matthew 5:25. The words state that you must, "agree with your adversary quickly, while you are on the way with him, lest your adversary deliver you to the judge, the judge hand you over to the officer, and you be thrown into prison." Because God is a God of justice and righteousness, if we sin and don't repent, the enemy has every right to not only accuse us, but he then has a key to your house, your spiritual house. He can then access you and what belongs to you and you can rebuke him all you like but he knows the law!

It's just like with squatters! In the UK, if squatters get access to your inside your home because you left a window open, or a door unlocked (which is your responsibility), you have hell – pardon the pun – to get them out! By law, "a long-term squatter can become the registered owner of property or land they've occupied without the owner's permission." Can you imagine? Your own house, that you own, someone can come in and take rightful ownership! In order for you to get them out, you have to go to the Courts! When I found that out, I was flabbergasted, but it's the law! It may even get to the point where you have to pay them to get out of your house! What a joke! But it all starts if they get access because of our own doing. As it is in the natural realm, so it is in the spirit realm! If we sin, without repentance, we give demonic squatters the right of access to our lives, and we then have to go through a whole legal process to evict them!

The Courts of Heaven

I am not even going to pretend I am an authority on this subject! But what I will say is that going to the courts and repenting of transgressions and going way back, to not just our sins, known and unknown, sins of omission and commission, but right back to our mother's mother's side and mother's father's side and the same on our father's side – clearing those grounds through repentance, coming into agreement with the enemy about my sin, and seeking God's forgiveness releases us from the legal right that he has to interfere with our lives and our destinies. As we sin daily, we must repent daily and do it quickly if we want to deny him this opportunity.

My personal experience of the power of the Courts of Heaven was receiving healing from my asthma. I have suffered from asthma since I was a young child. I have had inhalers for as long as I can remember and have never been able to do physical exercise without needing to rely on relievers (effectively steroids) to help regulate my breathing. In most cases, people grow out of asthma, but as I was getting older, my asthma was getting worse! I put it down to working in an area where there was a lot of pollution. The Catford gyratory

CHAPTER 8. WHERE DO WE GO FROM HERE?

in South East London, where I lived, was a smog-fest! You could basically taste all the carbon emissions and no doubt that could have certainly impacted this, but I believe the real root was the doors of unforgiveness that I had opened in my life, which gave the enemy legal squatters rights into my heart and my body. The more offense I continued to harbour, the more power he had over me. Going to the Courts one time, I repented, I released those who had hurt me, forgave myself for being hurt and kept it moving. My healing was almost instantaneous, and the squatter was evicted! But the one thing I realise about squatters, especially those in the kingdom of darkness, is that they will keep trying to find new ways back in! This is why buildings that are empty are securely boarded up with iron grates to prevent access from uninvited guests. The doors and windows of our lives need to be sealed and protected with the blood of Jesus and we will certainly need to be mindful of times where those grates automatically come down when we sin and fail to ask for forgiveness.

If you do need to go to the Courts of Heaven to defend yourself against claims made by our adversary "the accuser of the brethren" (Revelations 12:10), you need to do so with the support of your advocate, Jesus. Jesus is described as our advocate in 1 John 2:1. The Greek translation for "advocate", *parakletos*, also means *friend* and it literally means "someone who is "called to one's side," especially during a time of need." Can you imagine? Jesus will not only defend you but be there to totally have your back and be there for moral support! I'm still trying to study and learn more about this because I firmly believe it will be a source of great power and authority against the strategies of hell. When you don't know the law, you are vulnerable and believe me, the enemy knows the law inside out and God, who is just, has to uphold it!

Extreme Obedience

I don't think I have ever operated fully in extreme obedience to God with any passion and determination in the past. There was certainly a part of me that would follow instructions and rules out of a desire to people-please and not be seen to be being *rebellious* or *non-conformist*, to man…but in terms of my relationship with God, it was not the same.

I was more concerned about what other people would say, and their opinion than what God had wanted/required of me. Whether this was regarding a dress code, make-up, jewellery, music, whatever the area that I had been given an instruction or requirement, there was a pattern that I would never take it back to God, back to the Word of God and ask God and Holy Spirit what I was to do. I took the words, and the instruction of man ahead of God and any extreme obedience was to them. Not only was this very dangerous, but it is completely disrespectful to God and I have had to repent for that. I have had to repent for putting man's views and opinions ahead of God's. That cannot ever be the way things are done. God's desires and instructions should supersede everything, and I have learnt the hard way that failure to do that is actually sinful. I had made 'man' my God and that was plain and simple idolatry.

Now hear me, there is a balance. The Bible says, "Obey them that have the rule over you, and submit yourselves: for they watch for your souls, as they that must give account, that they may do it with joy, and not with grief: for that is unprofitable for you." (Hebrews 13:17) This clearly states that we need to respect and honour our leaders in the church and elsewhere, however, what trumps that is the instruction of the Lord. If you are told by God to do something, *that* has to come first and this may not always be the popular vote, or in line with what everyone else is doing, but that is why you have to be determined to operate in *extreme obedience*.

I have learnt not to second guess what God is saying to me. Initially, I wasn't sure if I was hearing His voice until I started seeing more and more confirmations. I started to realise that I was hearing the voice of God/Holy Spirit and that just like Jesus promised, He had left me a Counsellor that would be there to support me and guide me and ensure I'm making the right decisions. That did not take away, however, the doubt you wrestle with from time to time, that you may have got it wrong and you have to learn to just press through, knowing that God in His mercy, will guide you back on the right path should you stray.

Heavenly Mindset

Putting on the helmet of salvation three times daily for some weeks, really allowed me to embed the truth and recondition my mind to bring it in line with the word of God. The Bible already talked about this before it became trendy to *meditate* and retrain your thoughts, explaining to us in several scriptures, Proverbs 23:7 says, "As a man thinketh in his heart, so is he". If we didn't understand this before, understand now that your thoughts have power! When we operate thinking with our carnal minds that thoughts are just thoughts, we totally miss the mark and deny ourselves access to some of our most powerful spiritual weapons as well as think into existence some of our biggest doubts and fears. Romans 12:2 tells us that we should, "not copy the behaviour and customs of this world, but let God transform you into a new person by changing the way you think. Then you will learn to know God's Will for you, which is good and pleasing and perfect." This verse basically sets out that we can be totally transformed as a human being, by just changing the way that we think!

Mahatma Gandhi gave a very well-known adage that I want to quote here because unless we adopt a heavenly mindset, acknowledging that it all starts with the thought and this leads people on to very unpleasant consequences.

> 'Watch your thoughts, for they become your words
> Watch your words, for they become your actions
> Watch your actions, for they become your habits
> Watch your habits, for they become character
> Watch your character because it becomes your destiny!'

I think you'll agree that this is a very inspirational piece, but not only is it inspirational, it is true. If we do not get our thoughts right, we can either create or destroy our own destinies.

Until I did the 'helmet of salvation' part of putting on the armour of God, helping me throughout the day to remember that I can "take every thought captive and make them obedient to Christ" (2 Corinthians 10:5) and that my thoughts are subject to me and not the other way around, I found that I battled massively with thoughts. I would often doubt, fear, catastrophise and be beaten up by thoughts, many of which had not even happened! But learning to take those thoughts captive and think on only what is "pure, lovely and of good report" (Philippians 4:8) was a discipline that I had to learn and still have to practice implementing even today.

Speak Life

The other area of authority that I was not walking in, was the power of my words. We all know the famous scripture, that "death and life are in the power of the tongue" (Proverbs 18:21) and whilst I quoted this, I would often create vows with my words that put myself in bondage! The enemy would even make some negative and very destructive phrases common vernacular and conversation so that people would effectively curse themselves without even realising it! Common phrases such as:

"It's killing me!"

"I can't take it any more"

"I will never do/say…"

"I will never be able to do…"

"I'm really bad at…"

The above, to name but a few, are phrases that are speaking into the spirit realm and creating either life or death. When we speak negativity, we reap negativity and vice-versa!

I had to unlearn the negative thoughts as well as the negative speech because both things together were creating death and destruction on so many levels. The minute I started to take dominion in this area, I saw changes in outcomes and also even my own behaviours and beliefs. The more I spoke positively, the more I believed! The more I believed, the more miracles and positive outcomes I saw made manifest in my life!

As I close, I want to remind you all that sustaining a lifestyle like this is not natural to our flesh. The extreme discipline, self-denial, commitment, hard work and diligence that is required to continue to adhere to the suggestions in these pages is immense. However, I will say it is possible. I have not, by any stretch of the imagination, been able to maintain all of these elements without fault, but I have done my best and Father sees my heart. That is what he wants, "a broken spirit and a contrite heart, He will not despise." (Psalm 51:17) It goes without saying that we will fail, as I have reminded us earlier in this book, we have all "sinned and fallen short of the glory of God" (Romans 3:23), and while we are still in our earthly bodies, this is going to be repeated.

When an athlete loses a race, they evaluate their performance, work on their area of weakness and mitigate against failure in the future. They don't stop competing, they continue to push through to do better next time. That's what we all have to do, "fight the good fight of faith," (1 Timothy 6:12) and "pursue peace with all *people*, and holiness, without which no one will see the Lord." (Hebrews 12:14) Above all things, don't stop training, even if you've won a few events. With every missed practice, you lose some of your edge. The regression from a Christian on fire to an apostate is a very slow fade. The journey for most will begin with a lapse in spending time with God on a daily basis, then to minimising time and involvement in serving within your church, and it would not take long until you are too weak to fight and too indifferent to care. Let's get back to business – time for playing church is up!

Acknowledgements

Firstly, I have to give glory and honour to the Most High God for entrusting me with this book.

I am truly humbled to have been used in this way and I am grateful that I can be a vessel through which he can draw many others to Himself.

I also want to thank Somalia Brown, who you will hear about throughout this book. She is an incredibly powerful woman of God quietly tearing down principalities and powers that get in the way of her God-given mandates. I am eternally grateful for being taught how to retrain my mind to be in-line with the word of God but also how to have my own personal relationship with God and find my identity in Him.

I am hugely grateful to my ever-supportive husband, Adonye. He is amazing! I am truly blessed.

To my wonderful children, who God is using to help and teach me daily, I love you all.

To my prayer partners, Michelle Ferguson and Davinia Powell, thank you for holding me to account every week, and my friends and family in the Potter's House Church and my wider friends and sisters in the Arise Women community – you are all amazing.

God bless you!

About the Author

Natasha Orumbie is married to Adonye Orumbie and has three beautiful children from their marriage. She is a born-again Christian and warrior woman for God. She serves in her local congregation ministering in song and working with children in several different capacities.

She is a trained secondary school teacher of English, and a serial entrepreneur, currently making waves in the baking business world with her company N.O. Cakes R Better and her Baker Squad.

Conscious Dreams
PUBLISHING

Be the author of your own destiny

www.consciousdreamspublishing.com

info@consciousdreamspublishing.com

Let's connect

CPSIA information can be obtained
at www.ICGtesting.com
Printed in the USA
LVHW020129300421
686058LV00017B/1336